A Seed Grows

My First Look at a Plant's Life Cycle

DISCARD

Written by Pamela Hickman
Illustrated by Heather Collins

Kids Can Press

This is the seed

that Sam planted.

This is the stem
that grew from the seed
that Sam planted.

This is the flower
that bloomed on the stem,
that grew from the seed
that Sam planted.

This is the bee
that drank from the flower,
that bloomed on the stem,
that grew from the seed
that Sam planted.

This is the pollen
that was left by the bee,
that drank from the flower,
that bloomed on the stem,
that grew from the seed
that Sam planted.

This is the fruit

that was made with the pollen,

that was left by the bee,

that drank from the flower,

that bloomed on the stem,

that grew from the seed

that Sam planted.

These are the new seeds
that formed in the fruit,
that was made with the pollen,
that was left by the bee,
that drank from the flower,
that bloomed on the stem,
that grew from the seed
that Sam planted.

Yum!